Piano Sketches Duets

Vitalij Neugasimov

Book 2

5 easy to intermediate pieces for piano four-hands

Contents

Durations are given below each piece.

OXFORD
UNIVERSITY PRESS

Great Clarendon Street, Oxford OX2 6DP, United Kingdom

This collection © Oxford University Press 2017
Unauthorized arrangement or photocopying of this copyright material is ILLEGAL

Vitalij Neugasimov has asserted his right under the Copyright, Designs
and Patents Act, 1988, to be identified as the Composer of these Works

Impression: 1
ISBN 978–0–19–351766–0
Music and text origination by Katie Johnston
Printed in Great Britain on acid-free paper by Halstan & Co. Ltd, Amersham, Bucks.

Thank you so much to my sister Liudmila Neugasimova, an exceptional piano teacher, for her invaluable contribution, brilliant ideas, encouragement, and support.

Tarantella

Vitalij Neugasimov

* Players with small hands may wish to omit the upper octave.

Tarantella

Vitalij Neugasimov

Duration: c.2 mins

Russian Song

Vitalij Neugasimov

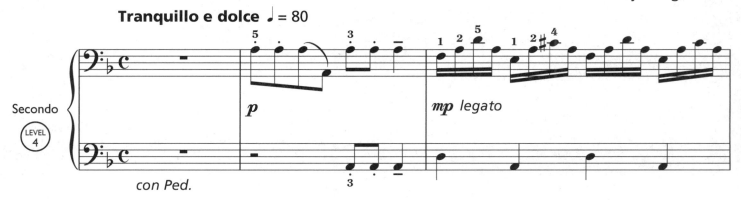

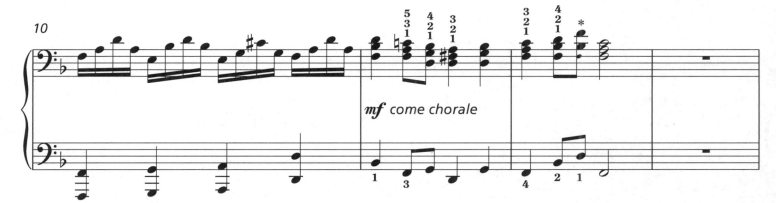

* Players with small hands may wish to omit the lower F.

Russian Song

Vitalij Neugasimov

Duration: c.1.5 mins

* Players with small hands may wish to omit the lower F.

Music for a Silent Film

Vitalij Neugasimov

Music for a Silent Film

Vitalij Neugasimov

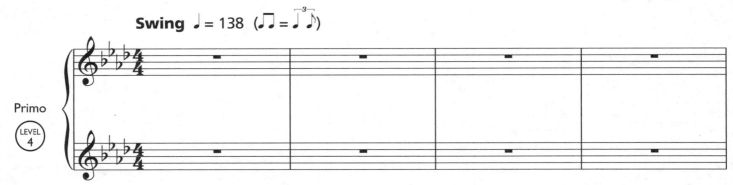

Primo
LEVEL 4

Duration: c.2 mins

Autumn in Paris

Autumn in Paris

Vitalij Neugasimov

Duration: c.2.5 mins

to my dearest friend Vytautas

Rumba for Johann

Vitalij Neugasimov

to my dearest friend Vytautas

Rumba for Johann

Vitalij Neugasimov

Duration: c.2 mins